Nan's sports car

"Beep! Beep!" It was Nan and Pop in Nan's sports car. She had just picked it up.

We all ran out to have
a look. It was flash! It
was painted bright red!

I said to Nan, "Can we hop in?"
Nan said, "Yes! Pop will hop
out and let you kids in."

Pop swung his legs out of the car, grabbed on and lifted himself up. Then he stood up and groaned.

The three of us jumped into the car. We checked it out. I said, "Look! I have a light." I turned it on.

"I have cooling back here!" said Nat.

Dan said, "I have a spot to put a drink."

"Look at this," said Nan. She pushed a button and the roof slid right back, letting the bright sun in. "Wow!" said Nat.

"Strap in, kids," said Nan. "Get set for some fun and the wind in your hair!"

Nan beeped her horn and took off down the street. "What speed can you go in this?" I said.

Nan said, "As quick as lightning, but I do the right thing and stick to the speed limit."

Nan took us into town.
She stopped at

the traffic lights and flashed
her lights just for fun.

She got us some drinks and then we started back. Her sports car was cool!

When we got back, Mum and Pop were waiting for us. We hopped out and Pop went to get in.

I said to Pop, "What do you think of Nan's sports car?"

Pop said, "I like the car. It's just that I have a problem with getting in and out!"

Words to blend

just	swung	grabbed
lifted	himself	jumped
spot	drink	slid
strap	wind	stick
stopped	traffic	flashed
went	problem	checked
turned	limit	roof

Before reading

Synopsis: Nan has a flash new sports car. She takes the children for a ride. They like it. So does Pop, although he has one problem with it.

Review graphemes/phonemes: or ai igh oo oa ee ar

Story discussion: Look at the cover and read the title together. Ask: *What do you think of Nan's sports car? Do you think it would be fun to go for a ride in it? What might happen in this story?*

Link to prior learning: Display a word with adjacent consonants from the story, e.g. *painted*. Ask children to put a dot under the single-letter graphemes (*p, n, t, e, d*) and a line under the digraph (*ai*). Model, if necessary, how to sound out and blend the sounds together to read the word. Repeat with another word from the story, e.g. *bright*, and encourage the children to sound out and blend the word independently.

Vocabulary check: cooling – on page 7, this word is used to mean air conditioning

Decoding practice: Turn to page 5. Point to the words *stood* and *groaned* and check that children can sound out and blend them.

Tricky word practice: Display the word *my* and ask children to point out the tricky part of the word (*y*, which makes the /igh/ sound). Ask children to find and read this word in the book. Practise writing and reading the word.

After reading

Apply learning: Ask: *Why do you think Pop groaned as he got out of the car on page 5?* (It was painful for him.)

Comprehension

- Who is in the sports car at the start of the story?

- Who does Nan take for a ride in the sports car?

- Where do they go?

Fluency

- Pick a page that most of the group read quite easily. Ask them to reread it with pace and expression. Model how to do this if necessary.

- In pairs, children could read the dialogue on page 4, taking a part each. Can they make it sound as if the characters are really talking?

- Practise reading the words on page 17.

Tricky words review

was	pushed	all
out	my	he
your	go	do
like	into	some
said	when	were